Also by Jeff Ryan

Chain Letters and Other Poems
Amazon Best-Seller

Available at Tinyurl.com/chainletterspoetry

"I think what sets this book apart is Ryan's stronger imagery and subversive sense of humor. Several of the pieces... struck my brain with just the right tone, and resonated for longer than I'd expected them to."

-Charles Haynes

"[Ryan]... shows shine and promise from the beginning."

-Samantha Ripley

"For 99 cents, how could you say no?"
-Jacelyn Szkrybalo

To Leave
Or Die
In Nashville

Poems from a New England Boy
In the South

Jeff Ryan

Broken Lamp Publishers
Nashville

Broken Lamp Publishers

PMB 354064
2301 Vanderbilt Place
Nashville, TN 37235

TO LEAVE OR DIE IN NASHVILLE. Copyright © 2012 by Jeff Ryan. All rights reserved, including the right to reproduce this book or portions thereof in any form whatsoever without written permission with the exception of brief quotations embodied in critical articles and reviews. For information, contact "Broken Lamp Publishers Rights Division" online at brokenlamppublishers@gmail.com

First edition published 2013.

Designed by Jeff Ryan

Ryan, Jeff.
To Leave or Die in Nashville: Poems from a New England Boy in the South/ by Jeff Ryan

ISBN-13: 978-0-615-73387-6 (pbk)
ISBN-10: 0-615-73387-5 (pbk)

To Elle

Contents

Back to Nashville	1
My Problem with Poetry	3
Harper	5
Love	6
You're Cute for a Drop of Water	8
Muse	9
To the Redheaded Girl I Met in a Bar in Nashville	10
Writing of the Disaster	11
About the Diary of a Young Girl	13
Sinking Soon	21
Promise	23
Inbox	24
E, again	25
On Poetry	26
Ghosts	27
Growing Up	29
Another Dedication	31
Crows, Revisited	33
Eyes Like Sapphires	36
An Ars Poetica	37
Motivation	39
To a Different Kind of Emily	40
LY	41
Jealousy	44
Tuesday Morning	45
Pretty Girls	46
The Gulf	49
JB	51
Have You Ever Loved?	52
Sext	53
Roanoke	55
Raspberry Girls	56
Printer's Alley	60
Hindsight	62

H	63
The Scale of Things as I See Them	65
Talent	68
Roses	69
Autumn	70
A Self-Portrait	73
Elle: A Prelude	75
Spaz	76
Evolution	80
Elle	82
To Leave or Die in Nashville	89
Epilogue	91

TO LEAVE OR DIE IN NASHVILLE

"There is nothing to writing.
All you do is sit down at a
typewriter and bleed."

-Ernest Hemingway

Jeff Ryan

Back to Nashville

We were a hundred miles
Into Pennsylvania
With the wind whipping
Through the car windows,
Crawling our way past
Cows and Farm country
That hadn't moved in
Centuries
When I pulled over
Saying something about how
We needed gasoline.

You started bitching
In that way you do
About how you wanted to
Get to Nashville so that
We could get some rest.
The way where you're bitching
But you don't really mean it.

I ignored it anyway and
Put the pump in the tank
Letting it fill, then I
Sat on a bench in the
Middle of Harrisburg
While you went inside the
Building to
Piss.

I wanna be in this,
I told you.
Here's this place you might
Never see again.
These tiny houses
With pastel sidings

To Leave or Die in Nashville

And thin streets
With neighbors that know
Neighbors
Who never leave.

You scoffed.
Christ
I hate traveling
Anywhere except New York.
At least there's stuff
In New York.
Out here,
There's nothing.
Nothing but hicks and idiots
And probably liberals, too.

I shook my head
And started the car
Though I made damn sure to
Take the long way
Back to the highway.

My Problem with Poetry

The problem with poetry
For me
Is that I don't get it.

People tell me
I have no flow
That my meters don't match
Or that I'm still
Finding
My voice.

That's probably fair.

But I read poems
By the "greats"
And I don't get what
The hype is about.
There's nothing exciting
About reading a poem
Five pages long about a
Turtle that crosses the road
Except it's not a turtle.
It's the American spirit
Persevering despite
Great obstacles.

I said it already:
Give it to me straight
And don't pretend later
That there was some
Grand design you were
Building to all along.

Of course
Plenty of amateurs are

Shit, too.
I must get
Five emails a week asking me
To read someone else's poetry
And give some advice.
As if I have a clue.
The only reason I respond
Is to see if maybe they do.

But here's a tip:
Nobody actually uses the word
Sylvan.

And don't get me started
On metaphors.
Say for example,
I want to write a poem about
Stress.
I can't just tell you
That I'm stressed
And then discuss
All the babbling inconsistencies
In my head.
No, a poem
Needs a metaphor
Like how I am a too-full plate
About to crack
From the heat of the
Microwave.

Show don't tell.
Show don't tell.
That's why I'm rubbish
At poetry.

Harper

I know you,
She says.
You're going to write
A poem about how
I fucked that other guy,
Aren't you?
And I tell her
No,
Of course not, baby.
That would be childish.

Love

Sometimes I think it would be interesting
If men in porn fell in love with
Their coworkers –
Like there's one beautiful girl in particular
That he works with all the time
But he's still too nervous
To tell her how he feels.

How he falls asleep
Thinking of the way
The sunlight would fall across
Her face while she's
Sitting in his kitchen on
A quiet Sunday morning.

Instead, right when she's done
Performing, the cameras
Finished filming and they're both
Standing there naked,
And the tiniest window of opportunity
Presents itself to him,
Instead of finally asking her if
She'd like to get coffee sometime
(Just the two of them)
He smiles awkwardly
And she pats him on the back
And congratulates him
On his performance before
Rinsing with mouthwash and
Putting her robe back on.

He just wants to make love
Just once with her.

He feels it worst when

Jeff Ryan

They do a scene together
Pretending it's their honeymoon
And he carries her over the
Threshold in her dress
And he could swear
He'd never seen her
Look more beautiful
Than in that moment
When she laughed
Like the bells
In the wind.

He couldn't help but kiss her –
Truly kiss her with his soul to hers.

A few weeks later
He's sitting in his room
With breath like mustard
And whiskey
When he downloads the scene
Off the internet
Crying just a little
And rewatching that one moment
Until he passes out, asleep.

You're Cute for a Drop of Water

Every goddamn person
Has their own goddamn story
Like a unique little snowflake
And I want to know <u>your</u>
Snowflake.

I want to know your crystals
And your curves
And I want to smile at your
Structure
And I want to be with you
Until the day you finally melt.

Muse

I wonder if it embarrasses you
That I write about you so often.
It probably wouldn't change anything
If you did.
I'd still love you
With everything I am
And I'd still long for you
And dream of what it would
Be like
To be with you.

The thing is
You make me want to write
Love poems in a way
No one else does.
You make me want to
Say I love you
And then not say
Anything after
Like maybe I don't
Want an answer back
Because that would end the story.

I wonder if you notice
All the references to you
That I place in between
My syllables.

Do you remember
What I remember?
And when I'm thinking of you
Are you thinking of me
Too?

To the Redheaded Girl I Met in a Bar in Nashville

Beer.
Some shots.
You keep moving closer
And I know you want to kiss me.

You're pretty
I tell you
Even though I know
You're not.

Truth be told
Your hairline is too high
And your voice would probably give
Me a headache if I had to
Listen to it all day
And you're drunker than I am
By a lot
So I'll probably feel guilty
About all this
Tomorrow.

Writing of the Disaster

You're taking words for granted
Just so you know.

That little of
Above in the title
For example.
It means twice what you think.

"A Prison gets to be a friend."
That gets means two things too.

A prison got to be your friend.
Your friend?
His friend?
Can you write a letter to a dead man?
Personalized to eyes
That will never see
Now that the maggots have been through with them?

"Hello"
You say.

"Hello"
I say.

But I will never know you.

You are other.
Some kind of vile
Butcher masquerading as a man.
Or perhaps you are truly
As boring as you look
In the old photographs.

They tell me you're evil.

To Leave or Die in Nashville

It is an act of clarification,
They tell me.

There's some degree of distortion though.
It's impossible to tell the story without it.

You are other.
A rapist who could have been a firefighter
Who could have been a soldier
Who could have been a hero.

Your death was the end of those possibilities.
Death was the end of every possibility
But you died before then.
You died when you first used the knife
(with two meanings).

You were dead
And your body was just
Waiting to catch up
And shut down.

I could forgive you.
Forgive you and damn you to
The condemnation of guilt
That it implies.

But you are dead
And the disaster has passed.
Adieu to the Butcher.

Jeff Ryan

About the Diary of a Young Girl

I.   To Another

There was a time when
I loved a little Polish girl
With lips like roses and
Skin soft as silk.

They made her dig
Her own grave then
They brought to light
All of their guns
And rained them down
On everyone
And when her body
Hit the ground
Her soul slipped out
And cried out loud
Then they poured dirt
Onto her face
As her soul flew
Out into space.
Now she's been sleeping
In the clouds
Or somewhere else
Where dreams are found.

II.   On Memory

I wonder what they would
Say if they could talk
The menorahs and Torahs
Tucked away in
European pawn shops.

Would the pewter and silver
Tell me about the time when
The men with armbands
Red as blood broke in and
Beat her father until his
Teeth chipped and fell
Into the floorboards?
Would they betray his
Secret hiding under the
Stairs inside the back
Cupboard covered by wallpaper
And a broom?
Would they record in their
Shine the way she cried
When she heard them screaming
Or her helplessness to
Stop it all?

Because I'd rather not hear that
Story.
I'm sure you understand.

III. On Disappointment

The Canadians came down from the sky
Like gray angels with
Giant parachute wings
And you all wanted to cheer
For salvation so close.
The Allies in your city
About to rescue you
And make your life
Normal and make it
Yours once again.

Until you saw the angels
Get rounded up like tigers
In the zoo
And thrown into the van.

You stayed quivering
In your hidden crevice
Not daring to cry so that
They wouldn't round you up
Too.

To Leave or Die in Nashville

IV.   On Love

Do you remember the room
Where you would slide in
Beside me, all legs and breasts?
And do you remember the way
Our bodies intertwined like
The threads of rope from a
Noose hanging in the ghetto?

The embraces snuck behind
Bread baskets and fruit stands
Dodging Gestapo and swearing
We could hide forever.

You were all legs and breasts
Laughing outside of every
Line I could ever write.
And we were out
In the fields laying together,
Laughing under the sky
When they came looking
To pull us up out of the Earth and
Harvest us like heads of lettuce.

Even as we sit, emaciated in
Separate work camps lingering
Until a cold shower
Ends our day
And every day after that
I think of you.

Even then
As I carry stones into piles
And dream about the next time I'll
Hold you again if I'll ever
Hold you again.

Jeff Ryan

I won't let them take the
Ghost of you from my memory.

Stay with me always.

V.   On Childhood

You once were a princess and
Your father put peach
Blossoms in your hair
And built you a castle that
Climbed into the clouds.

You and Jozef and I
Would run together and
Tell secrets whispered in
Alleyways and steal apples
To eat for fun
Back in the days when there
Were still apples to eat.

Jozef was always the fastest
And got the most thrill from
Thieving and storing his treasures in
The basement of your mother's house.
We would tell him to be good
And tell him to stop
But secretly we loved the thrill too
And lived with him inside those
Moments of exhilaration.

Jozef was always the fastest so when
The train unloaded and
The men with guns told him it was a race,
Told all of us it was a race, to the
Albreit Macht Frei
He believed it and believed
His legs would save his life
And if he did what they said
He believed that
Maybe he would get through this and
Get back to his alleys and his fun

Jeff Ryan

And the field where he would sit
And pick flowers
And dream.

He didn't realize his mistake until they
Led him and all the other boys and men
Who won the race into a room that
Filled with gas. Not until his eyes
Rolled back into his head and
Poisoned froth came choking out of his throat.

We didn't know that, you and I
Because we were still on the train.
Even though they told us to separate.
I didn't want to leave you
Scared and tired and beautiful
Without telling you
I love you.
Without gathering what
Peach blossoms I could find
And making them into a crown for you.

Though now they are rotted and
The only thing keeping you breathing
Is stale bread pushed through
A hole in a wall by your mother,
Though your castle was built too high
So that when your sister tumbled from the top
She died when she hit the Earth.

One day they will burn your body
Cold and lifeless
In a heap with all the other bodies
And even while the fire burns
The world will grow
Colder.

I will miss you always.

VI. On Rebuilding

There isn't much to say these days
Walking within the rubble of Warsaw
Using stone and wood for blankets
And shattered glass for pillows.

A Polish man – a Lutheran
Lives in your house now
And his children laugh
Whenever I mention your name.
They call it their house
And they paint your walls
And piss in your toilet
And sleep in your bed.

In the rooms where I first
Discovered your body
And the way it moved with mine
He now mates with his wife.
You can hear them most nights
Squawking and howling
Like chimpanzees.

After Auschwitz there isn't
Much to talk about
Except that you
Will never smile again

And that I will miss you always.

Jeff Ryan

Sinking Soon

One time we drove
All the way to the coast
To see the ships
That once held
Sailors and whales
And that still told
Stories centuries-old
If you stopped to listen closely enough
To the rocking on the waves.

And right in the middle
When I was starting to
Get lost in colonial legacy
You started whining about the heat,
About how you wanted to go because
You don't have any history in your soul
And it's a lot easier to leave when
You weren't the one paying for
Both tickets.

The fight fizzled when I realized
That none of it mattered.
We'd reached the moment when I knew
I wouldn't love you forever
And that it was only a matter of time
Before we dashed our own boat
To bits on the rocks.

So like a ship at sea
You wanted to be alone.
But how long can you hold
With a whole in your hull
Till the sea worms
Find the sailors
And hollow out their eyes

To Leave or Die in Nashville

Drowning softly
In cold waters
On a burning day
In May?

Promise

Across a river
And across a mountain
I threw a nickel
In a fountain

And wished
For something secret
And a place
Where I could keep it

Like the secret song
Before you sleep;
A ritual,
Like counting sheep.

Well, I'll sleep out
In the gutter
If you'll just sleep
On my floor

And when I leave you
In the morning
I'll forget to
Lock my door.

If you stayed
You'd be my lover
And love all
That I have left.

Inbox

I must have gotten
Ten emails in the last
Three days.
For sales
Playing limbo with
Discounts
And I'm like

Hello
That's very nice of you
To offer me 40% off
And free domestic shipping
But could you please do it
When I'm not scraping
Together my dollars
So I can have enough
Money to pay for
Tuition and food and beer.
You know, the things I
Actually need?

It's like
I'll buy it when I finally
Have some cash.

Hopefully soon,
I promise.

E, again

I should put it all
Behind me.

That would be the
Smart
thing to do.

It was a love story

& all that's left to
do
Is tell it
one more time.

A quiet afternoon.

Suddenly
A year passes.

Another lesson
Learned the hard way.

And even if it didn't matter
In the end
The point is

Love

& Me
      mory.

On Poetry

I'm drunk so it's easy to make my letters and sounds blend like pictures or sketches as they paint the scenes of places I've never been and girls I've only dreamed of loving.

And it flows.

Ghosts

I can't remember how all these visions
Got stuck inside my head.
All these dreams swirling in my
Atmosphere and clogging
My sleep in my bed.

The ghosts filling up the walls inside my room
And knocking on my window
With pebbles from my yard.

Yeah, I know something of ghosts
When I've been awake long enough
To forget what sleep means.

My living room is filled
With the ghost of an uncertain bride
Who waltzes through my life and
Laughs every time I say I'm lonely.
Who kisses my cheek with love.

Or rather it's an empty heart and an
Empty hand in a
Hollow house called
Home.

It's a bit too late to give up
And go back to how things used to be.
I don't even know what I could
Do with my life
Or what I would.
The only thing I know for
Sure these days

(Past the drug-induced haze
After too many sleepless nights

And pill-sponsored mornings
That last long past nightfall)

Is my name.
It's a start and a push in
The proper direction.
Which is away from all my demons
Who somehow all look just like you.

I might be going insane
But being crazy
Is the least of my worries.
Either way I hope I
Finish this book in time
Because it would be nice
To leave a little token
To remember me by
Printed on paper over
Attempts of lesser men.

And little ghost
Living in my living room
Tell me don't give up
No I won't give up
Are you alive
Because I feel alive
And in my blood
I'm bleeding ink
And dreams
And in between these lines
Is the sound of souls on
Fire
But not burning.
Can you hear it too?

Growing Up

I've got this strange disease
That makes me seem to think
I'm going to marry every girl
That I meet.

When I'm walking down the street
I'm always dropping to one knee
'Cuz I think that this girl
Might be the one.

It's just that every girl is pretty
And every girl's so witty.
What the hell am I
Supposed to do?

I can't sleep correctly
And I can't think of anything
To make these thoughts of her
Go away.

I have ninety-nine problems
And you count as one.
I've got a leg that hurts all the time
But I swear that I am fine.

Yes I swear that I am fine.

(Bullshit I'm not okay
I'm miserable
With this stupid life that
I have chosen.

I just need to get paid
Get laid

To Leave or Die in Nashville

And make a few million
Dollars

So I can buy a house in Malibu
Have a wait staff
And a butler too
Marry a few hundred
Different wives
And then get in an affair
With my maid instead).

I am definitely crazy.
I swear that I am
I am fine
But we both know that
It's a lie.

There's a man who tells me
To take my pills
Every night before I go
To sleep.

I don't because they take
The edge off my loneliness,
And then I'd have nothing to write.

And then I'd be nothing at all.

Another Dedication

If I have my way
A lot of people are going
To read
This book.

The one you're holding
In your hands.

The one
That was
Dedicated
To you
Back before everything went to
Shit.

They'll read it
And I hope that they
Enjoy it
And I hope that they
Relate
And think

That poem makes
Sense
To me
And I feel those things
Too.

They'll relate
But they'll never
Get it.
They'll never understand.
Not like you do.
I need you to realize.
I put these words

To Leave or Die in Nashville

Down on paper
With your face
In my mind
The whole time.

Everyone else
Will relate.
They'll relate
And they'll read it
And they'll think they
Understand.

And maybe some
Will get close.

But never really.
Not like you.

They'll never remember
That night in November
When we walked together
Through campus
And got lost in a
Parking lot.
And they'll never get mad
Because they really believed
That I knew what I was
Talking about
When I told them about
The stars.

Just remember.
It's for you.

Crows, Revisited

I miss those stupid fuckers
Even after they
Kicked me
Like a dog
And left me to die
In the middle of the road
(Metaphorically speaking).

I miss growing up
Sometimes lonely
By train tracks and a highway
And a river where every day
I'd dream of recognition.
Going through childhood
With nostalgia
For an invented homeland
Where my heroism knew
No bounds.

I miss the way we would
Walk around town
Because there never was
Anything new
And I miss the way
We would sit around in
Basements
Doing the same old things
We always did
Which usually
Was nothing
At all.

We'd scrape away for minutes
Carved from October evenings
Sitting on lawns

To Leave or Die in Nashville

And breathing in that
Dry cold air
Until our lips chapped
And our ears burned,
Playing games like
Who am I?
And
What Will I Be?

I wonder if they remember
How once upon a time
We were all young together
And our dreams grew on
Trees just like we thought
Money would.

I doubt they remember me
Any more,
Or think about me
Like this.

But I miss the days
Before they were crows,
Back when we would
Come up with excuses
Just to call up our crushes
And somehow swallow enough
Courage to keep up
A conversation about
Chemistry or math or
Stuff that was on our minds.

I don't know why
Things changed.
Why my phone
Rang less and less
Until eventually
It stopped ringing

At all.

I left in shame
Filled with hate,
A New England boy
Fleeing south to some place
Where none of them
Would be.

And sometimes their lives
Come up in pictures when
I'm sure that no one else
Is watching me.
I can't help but notice that
Their faces don't look
Like the faces of my friends
Any more.
More like the faces of
Actors in movies
I watched when I was younger.
Familiar
Yet Foreign.

But even still
Some nights when
My flight hits
In just the right places
All of a sudden
I'll miss everyone.
Even the beaks and feathers
Of the crows.

Eyes Like Sapphires

I once met a girl
With eyes like
Sapphires
And a body that could
Make men
Go Mad.

And once she told me
While running her finger across my chest
That you could tell a lot
About a person
By what they kept
Next to their bed.

At the time I just
Laughed and
Kissed her
And squeezed that body
That could make men
Go Mad.

But she was on to something.

Next to my bed
Are some empty
Beer bottles
And a half-eaten bag
Of crackers
And those little black books
I keep all my poems in
And I think I had a condom
At some point.
But I probably lost it.

Jeff Ryan

An Ars Poetica

You can't talk to a poet.
Not really.

Every time you
Start to get close
You have to wonder if
They're going to put it
In a book and
Plaster your name and your
Memories onto a
Piece of paper
For the whole world to
Read.

I won't lie,
It's a valid fear.
I do it myself.

Every time you share
A secret or a
Beautiful moment
You have to wonder if a poet is
Sitting there
With you
Embracing it
Or if he's off
In another world
Thinking of how to
Take these thoughts and
Feelings and
Bottle them up into
Syllables or images
Until that private moment
Holding hands in a field
On a Sunday afternoon

To Leave or Die in Nashville

Isn't so private
And a thousand other people
Are there next to you
Poking it and
Prodding it and
Taking all the special from it.

Do not become a writer
If you are not willing
To have your friends
Keep quiet around you
Or have your lovers
Leave a little piece
Of themselves
A secret from you.

And most certainly
Do not become a poet
Because then you
Will suffer the same
As a writer does
Only no one will be
Buying
Your books.

Motivation

She told me
All the best poets
Were dead
From bar fights
And bleeding
And too many nights spent
Drinking
Instead of sleeping
So there wasn't any point
In keeping all this up.
The best who'd ever written
Were already in their graves.

I told her I was doing
The best I could
Given the resources that
I had.

To a Different Kind of Emily

I once made love to a
Porn star.
Our spirits intertwined in
A journey
Of self-discovery devoted to
Pleasure and
The exploration of
Sensation.

I'm just kidding.
I fucked her twice
And never called her back
And that was that.

Jeff Ryan

LY

I want to kiss you.

I can't stop writing
Poems
Because I want to
Write them about you.

I want to kiss you
Like a squirrel
Running around for
Reasons it couldn't explain
And bunching all the acorns up into
The hollow of a tree.
Would you like to
Be a squirrel with me
In the hollow of a tree?

Would you like to kiss
In the rain like a fancy
Movie?
I could spin you around
And pretend it's the
First time I've seen you
In months.
Except it actually is
So I wouldn't have to
Pretend much.

Would you want
To kiss at all?
Because
You make me want to
Take up smoking
Just so I could
Offer you my last

To Leave or Die in Nashville

Cigarette and give it to
You as suave as I
Can,
Like James Bond maybe.
And then after I could
Hold your hand
In my car
Or take the long
Way to your house.

Do you think that we
Could stare into people's
Houses again?

Because I like you.

I like you so much
I forgot the metaphor.

I can't believe I
Called you a squirrel.
That's not even
Cute.

I hope that doesn't
Make you think I'm
Weird.

I'm a little bit weird.

But I want to spend
Time with you.
Like let's hang out
And get ice cream
Or let's don't since you're
Allergic.

Let's take a kayak instead

Jeff Ryan

Into the middle of a lake
And find a talking fish
Who will sing to us
And grant wishes.

And can I kiss you yet?
Because what I'm
Getting at is that
I want to.
I really do.

Jealousy

Someone is waiting
& trying to love you
& kiss you
& steal you from the skies
But I'll shoot them
If I have to
& keep you always
In my eyes.

Tuesday Morning

Got a book deadline
Fast approaching in between
Classes and exams and
Responsibilities.
Can't write any poems
Right now.
Too fucking tired.
Went to sleep
At 4AM
Because

I was up all night
Talking to a pretty girl
With fire in her hair
And winging for my friend
Who had met a much prettier girl
(That's just how it goes).

Woke up too early
To be here now
Learning
About cortar-ing el césped.
Some bullshit.
Got a deadline
To meet.
This will have to do.

Pretty Girls

"I'm just telling you,"
He says,
Slurring words and staring
Nowhere in particular.

"I'm just telling you
There are pretty girls
Everywhere you go.
You couldn't even learn
All their names
If you tried.
Like
I swear to god
One time I met
This beautiful girl
Named Olga.
Who's ever heard of a
Pretty Olga?
But there she was
Clear as day
And hot as hell."

I started telling him
I knew that all along
Before he cut me off.

"Of course
You did. You're a goddamn
Romantic.
Do you think you've ever been in
Love?

I told him
I didn't really think so.

"Bullshit you haven't.
You fall in love all the time.
I even know her
Name
But I'm not going to
Embarrass you
By saying it
Right now."

I asked him what his
Point was.

"I have this theory
That I wanted to
Test on you
Because you love so much.
I have a
Theory.
I think that you're not
In love
With a woman; that is
I think you're finally
Over her and
Moved on and
Don't give a rat's ass about her life
Once you can't
Remember what her
Tits look like
Anymore."

I thought about my high school girlfriend.
I certainly couldn't remember her tits.
Or her phone number.
Or what she was doing with her life these days.

Good riddance.

We used to tell

To Leave or Die in Nashville

Each other that we could
Make it through
Anything.
That we'd be together
Until the very end.
Then she started
Meeting other guys
In the naked sense
And took her time in
Letting me know
That I was only a
Stupid kid
She used to fool around with.

It ended quickly after that.
After I made a
Fool of myself.
Before I realized there were
Pretty girls everywhere
And you couldn't remember
All their names
If you tried.

The Gulf

I

Sitting on a beach
Looking at a small town moon
Could we kiss each other clean
Underneath a Thursday sky
Because I'm thinking
That I miss you
And I wish you'd get here soon.
I loved you on a Thursday
Underneath a Thursday moon

II

There are faces in the sand.

Pockets and rivets and craters
That turn from
Eye sockets into mouths
And they're screaming at me
Saying what do you
Want to be
And do you think you're any good?
You'll never keep this up
When you get drunker
Than you should.
Everyone grows up
Sometime and we
Hope that you catch up.

III

I must have said it a thousand times
That I want to run away
From here and shut off my

To Leave or Die in Nashville

Phone and live someplace else
Where I can be a person that
No one else knows

But this small town sky
Won't let me go.

JB

I don't think you can
Ever really know how
Much you love the
Way a girl smiles until
She tells you that
She wants the last words
You ever hear from her
To be
I hate you.

Have You Ever Loved?

Have you ever loved
Like a witch driving
Thirty miles an hour
Over the speed limit
On the interstate
Out by Tulsa
But when the trooper
Pulls her over
She vanishes
Like so much mist
Under a blue moon?

Sext

Sext: I want to untie your shoelaces
So that you'll trip
And maybe then you'll fall for me.

Except I hope you don't get hurt.
I don't want you to get hurt.

Instead I hope you'll sleep with me
Because I want to sleep with you.
But like
Actually fall asleep with you.
Like actually what I want
Is to go unconscious
With your body
Next to my body
And then regain consciousness
With your body still
Next to my body.

I want to kiss you on your cheek
Until your eyes open
Just enough for you to be
Just barely aware of your
Surroundings.
Enough to recognize me
And the instant you do
And the instant you start to smile
I want to kiss you on the lips.

I want to kiss you on your face
And then I want to whisper clichés
Into your ear.
I want to tell you that
You do to me
What sunlight does to flowers.

To Leave or Die in Nashville

You do to me
What cherry-flavored cough syrup
Does to people who have coughs.

You make me smile.

I like smiling with you
I like kissing you.
I like stars.
I want to count stars with you.
I want to kiss you
Under all the stars.

I want to kiss you and never stop.

I want to kiss you in an elevator
When there are no people around
Or maybe sometimes when there are
But only on the cheek maybe
Because we are both kind of
Private people.

But still I had to
Throw this together because
This book wouldn't be right
Without you in it.

Jeff Ryan

Roanoke

In Roanoke
Slowly coming to the realization that
Settling in America was a bad idea.
Starving, freezing, scared
Wondering idly whether it
Would be easier to die
From natives or from weather
And whether it would be
Frowned upon to let the
Crying baby die in the
Night, just for some
Peace and Quiet.

In Roanoke
Where the people are
Complaining and sniffling and grumbling
With shivers in their backs
And snot in their noses
And fighting with each other all the time
Just like all the people
We know now.

Raspberry Girls

I remember the first girl I ever kissed
Tasted like raspberries. She
Made my brain set off
Explosions and fireworks and dynamite
And I never wanted to let her go or end that kiss.

Her name was Michelle and she was
The kind of girl that made boys want to
Learn about space and become
Astronauts and walk around on the moon
Just so they could look back across the empty black of
the universe
To smile at the continents floating on a little blue dot.

I remember our story
Just like I remember all the stories from
People that have changed who I am.

I remember that the day when we first kissed
She gave me a letter she'd written.
It was typed and smudged because
She was so nervous to give it to me
She ripped it from the printer
Before the ink had the chance to dry.
I must have read that letter
A million times and I'll remember
It forever just like you're supposed
To remember the first time
Someone cares about you.

And because she gave a little piece of herself
I wanted to give a little piece of me back
So I wrote her a letter about something
My fifth grade teacher told me.
How if you drop a paper and a

Jeff Ryan

Piano off the Leaning Tower of Pisa
They'll hit the ground at the
Same time and fall at the
Same speed – technically.
In reality air resistance will take over
And the piano will fall a lot faster
And shatter on impact into
A mess of ivory and firewood
While the paper floats on the breeze.

People are kind of like that too, I told her.

When people fall in love
They do it at different rates and sometimes
They shatter at different times and the
Whole process can get messy
Even if she tastes like
Raspberries when she kisses you.

Her mother found the letter that I wrote
Hidden between some couch cushions,
Threw it away and told Michelle to
Never talk to me again because 12 years
Is too few to know anything about
Love.

In hindsight that turned out to be correct
But then again if there's an age that exists
When you learn what love means
I've yet to find it out.

The second girl I ever kissed tasted like
Menthol cigarettes which sounds like a complaint
Though I didn't mind.
Beggars can't be choosers after all
And I guess there are only so many
Raspberry girls in the world.

To Leave or Die in Nashville

She lived in the trailer park
Down the street
And dared me to touch her breasts
One time when her mother wasn't home.
I told her that I must have
Kissed her wrong.

It's not like I'm going to
Stop looking for another girl
With raspberry on her lips.
Every kiss along the way has a story
And over time those stories
Have all become memories.

I'm still trying to figure out how to take
All of this life that I have and
Put it down onto paper without losing
Any of the details. I'm scared to
Write myself into a book that
You can smell or hold
Because I'm worried that the
Story won't unfold into verses
And I can't rhyme my poems
Because I don't know how to force the past
Into sounds that work pretty together.

But if I could talk to Michelle
One more time
I'd let her know that things are
Supposed to get dirty,
Supposed to shatter
And that I didn't mind when
She hurt me
Because if she hadn't then I
Wouldn't have known.
I'm not sad I said I loved you
Before we both knew what love was.

Back then all I really cared about was raspberries.

Printer's Alley

At the bar you asked if I
Were lonely ever and
I said that it was impossible
In a city this friendly.
Even the pigeons would talk
If you tilted your head
Just right.

That's true but not the whole truth
Because people talk no problem
In a city as warm as this
But when they talk about the weather
They become nothing but
Interchangeable pieces
And I don't bother with the
Energy to tell any of them
Apart.

There are more important things
Than dolls' names.

So it ends up that I find myself sitting
More often than not
With a bottle in each hand
And a bartender
Who loves me more and more
As the night goes on.

Then I walk through the
Lit streets of Nashville and a
Campus like a parkway and when
I'm there alone at that hour
You'd be surprised about how
You can't hear the traffic or
The shouting or loud music

Jeff Ryan

From talented people who are
Waiting for excuses to give
Up on their dreams.

There's usually one just
Around the corner if you're
Willing to work for it
A bit.

Back last winter someone asked me
What I did with my life.
I told her I sleep and
Pick up girls in bars and
Sometimes write poems
But mostly I drink.
She laughed a bit too hard and
I kept scanning the rest of the bar
Looking for someone else to
Talk to.

I ended up taking her
Home anyways.
It's a numbers game
And my roommate's ego gets
Too big when he notices
There hasn't been a new girl
In my bed in a while.

Hindsight

She told me what we had was over
And that she never wanted to be
My friend again
That I was disrespectful
And she deserved much better than me,
Which was true.
Then she started listing
All the things she hated about me,
A projectile that picked up speed with
Every word it used
And shot me in my lung
So that when she asked me
If I had anything to say for myself
For once
I didn't.
Nothing
Witty or
Heartfelt or
True.
And even afterwards
While I was walking down the stairs alone
Expecting l'espirit de l'escalier,
The perfect response that would
Win her back or at least make her
Not hate me so much,
I still couldn't think of anything
To say for myself except
I'm sure I'll miss her someday.

Jeff Ryan

H

I met you by a fire
Toasting marshmallows and
Making smores and
You asked me if I could
Make one for you.

I said of course
Because I thought you
Were the prettiest girl
In the room.

I'm starting to notice that
You're the prettiest girl
In any room that I
Go into these days.

Even the ones you're not in.

Recently I've been
Distracted all the time
Hoping that I'll run into you
And that you'll smile
And notice me too.

And my heart keeps pumping
Images of your smile into
My bloodstream and my brain.

My friends ask me what you look like
So they can figure out what the
Big deal is.
They want to know
Why all of a sudden the
Only girl I ever talk about
Is you.

To Leave or Die in Nashville

I almost said that you look like Emma Stone
Only with brown hair instead of blonde
And you sort of have a longer face
And fewer freckles.
But the more I think about it I remember that
You don't really look like Emma Stone at all.

You're kind of like
The first time I ever
Flew in an airplane
Back when I was five or six
And got above the clouds and
Wondered what it would be like
To swim onto them
Between the sun and the sky.
And you're kind of like
The thrill of the take-off
When my body left the
Earth for the first time
Or maybe the adrenaline of landing
On the tarmac when the brakes deploy
Like a roller coaster.

That's what you look like
To me.
In a way that I've never seen
Anyone else look like before,
You're beautiful.

Jeff Ryan

The Scale of Things as I See Them

This is known though hard to comprehend
That there are more atoms in a
Grain of sand
Than there are grains of sand
On the planet Earth
And more molecules of water
In just one cup
Than cups of water in
All the oceans in the world.

There are more stars in the universe
Than you could count in one life
And all those stars have planets
With sand or something similar
Which means a lot of atoms
Exist out there.

And then remember that the universe is greater than
Infinity and somehow still expanding.

It's big.

So big that everything that's ever
Happened will one day be forgotten
Or never be known at all.
Even the flag on the moon
Has been bleached white by time.
Even a supernova and the
Explosion of a solar system
Or an entire galaxy devoured by
Black holes
Matters about as much
As forgetting to do your homework
Or a crush who doesn't know your name.

To Leave or Die in Nashville

Within infinity these things
Are pretty much the same.

When we look up at the
Same night sky and I see
Stardust glitter in your eye
You've got to remember
Yeah you've got to believe
That those stars travelled
Millions of years just to be
With you tonight.
And that matters as much
As when I drive fifteen minutes on
A stretch of interstate
To see you smile.

Against the backdrop of existence
We're small as ants.
But to say that even within
The scope of the universe
That a normal person like
You or Me
Cannot make an impact
Is simply wrong.

Brushing your teeth is pretty
Much a miracle when you think
Of the billions of people
You could have been
Or the infinite number of
Ways you might never have been.

Like if your ancestor living on
A German farm in 1433 had caught a
Cold and coughed himself to death
Instead of letting you get born,
For just one example.
Of course none of the rest of

Jeff Ryan

Us would have noticed the difference.
On the scale of infinity you matter
As much as a dying star
Coughing out its last rays
Of light
Or as much as an ant
Lost on its way home.

But a cup of water is a miracle
And the life of a star is a miracle
And brushing your teeth is a miracle
If you know how to look at it, too.

Talent

Van Gogh cut his ear off for
A lover who didn't want it
And Plath took a giant whiff of
Oven fumes
But for Wiesel it was probably
More pain to avoid the oven
While Hemingway splashed
Bits of his brains into his
Morning coffee.

We're all just looking for attention
In our own special way.

Roses

Officer Thompson shoves
A grainy photograph across
The desk.
"Was this your friend?"

I nod.

"I'm sorry," he whispers,
His badge glinting under
The buzz of an incandescent bulb.

"This city is killing me,"
I remember he had said one day
When we were alone.
"Corroded roses and
Rusted metal and
Snakes inside my skin.
A pulsing coursing heartbeat
Waiting for something to come,
But we're as blind as prayers
To see it around the corner."

I think it was a warning.

Thompson writes something down.
In his notepad.

Cause of death: An absence of hope
And a few too many gulps
Of Jim Beam.
He'd jumped,
With the concrete smiling below.

Autumn

I'm pounding another beer
Even though I'm already
So drunk that my vision
Is blurry
When I start thinking about you.
I haven't thought about you
In a long time.
Not since a few years back when
I met your parents and
Kissed you behind a playground
Because bangs are cute
And you made me laugh.

I used to love driving down
Highways lit up by headlights
To see you because
You didn't know who I was
And I didn't either
So it took all the pressure off.
It's been a while
But I've heard from someone
You're still pretty
And I remember that I spent
A lot of days dreaming about you.

There was a chill in the air
That night when we sat
On swings
Daring each other
To touch.
I asked if you believed
In ghosts because I didn't know
What else to say.

Jeff Ryan

I wanted to tell you
How this is where I live
In Autumn nights underneath
A ruddy-faced moon
And white stars that shine
Just like quarters at the
Bottom of a wishing well.

I wanted you to listen.
I wanted you to hear
The quiet steps from phantoms
Making their way between
Bushes across a New England
Farm town.
I wanted to know if you
Could hear the leaves grow
Tired from the frost and hear
Them die and hear them
Break for the ground.

I wanted to know if you could hear ghosts
So maybe then you could hear me
Chained down by memories
In a town where I
Used to own the streets.
Now there are new people
I don't recognize
Walking through the
Places I used to be
And other people holding hands
In the cornfield where
I first made love.

There used to be magic here
Back in those high school days.
In Tennessee I say that I'm fine
But I don't know if I'm ok.

To Leave or Die in Nashville

Except for when
We're driving in my car
Through this little town street.
Even though it's been a season
We haven't missed a beat.
If it weren't for you
I'd never leave the south
To come back to these scene.
For you I'll make
The exception.

I'm running red lights
Cuz I can't stop looking at you
Laughing out the window
With the wind in the air
Letting the breeze
Brush the autumn in your hair.

It's almost like
I'm my old self again.
If I knew who
That was to begin with.

I think it begins with you.

Jeff Ryan

A Self-Portrait

I have an itch.

I have an itch and it itches
And mother of fuck I have to scratch it
Because it's digging under my skin
And burning straight to my bones
And the instant I start scratching
My skin runs dry
And I start to bleed
Until I'm tearing up pieces of my flesh
And now I'm running but
Who decided to make the world
Move so
Goddamn
Slow
Minutes stretching into eons
But suddenly ending in seconds.

My brain is firing ideas
Like machine gun bullets
And my hands can't keep up
Because my axons are working much too
Slowly.

God created Heaven and
Had to rest on the seventh day
But I've done just as much
And couldn't sleep now if I tried.

Then the itch is gone
And is replaced
With nothing.
Nothing
But an emptiness
That takes up my whole body

And why hasn't anyone noticed
That my chest
Is gone
And in its place
Is only blank space.

The entirety
Of my personality
Was replaced with
A blank piece of paper.
But paper
Because that would be something
And what's in me is
Nothing.
Though I'm not quite sure
What changed
Or why I can't
Even leave
My bed.

Elle: A Prelude

Wake up
And run your fingers through
My hair and my face
And admire the space
Between our bodies
On the bed.

Let me pull your self close
Because I'm glad you're alive
Right here with me.

I remember when we
Found you
Carving crucifixes into your arms
Letting blood spill from the
Paleness of your skin like
Roses from the snow.

You were soaked inside your clothes
Saying "Sorry" to the floor
But there's no sorrow
To be sorry for
Because somehow
You survived.

You were hoping none would find you
But of course we all did find you
I just wish you could have known
That the stinging in your chest
Matched precisely with my own.

So press yourself
Against life
Because I'm
Glad you didn't die.

Spaz

Back in the 3rd grade
I used to have this problem
Where my arm would twitch
And my lip would turn to pins
And needles only if pins and needles
Were really bee stings and spider bites
And the world would sort of
Get up and leave me.

I used to think it happened to
Everyone. That is, until it happened
To me in class and I drooled on
Myself and everyone thought
It was the funniest thing
They'd ever seen.

When it started happening
The next day during gym class
I tried to excuse myself
Only the teacher wouldn't let me.
Instead he let me drool and twitch
Which the other kids soon noticed
And when the girl who was closest
Raised her hand to point it out
My gym teacher called me "Spaz."

It turns out that doesn't happen
To everyone and when it does
It's called a seizure. But the name Spaz stuck
Until the next big thing.

If there's one thing I've learned
From living on this Earth,
It's that you're
Never the only one.

Jeff Ryan

In 9th grade I was friends
With a barrel of nitroglycerine
Named DJ and he taught me
To listen to all the things
Being said that weren't words
In the conversation, because
Those usually mattered more.

DJ went home to his grandfather
Who would yell at us when we smoked
Cigarettes in church parking lots
And rode our skateboards
On the town hall
And as far as whatever happened
To his parents
I never asked
Because I never needed to know.

Except for the time
DJ was sent home
Because he beat a kid unconscious
When the kid said "suck it up."

Suck it up.

As if depression is something
That can be dismissed if you just
Deny that it exists
And not something that insists on
Becoming the very center of your being.
Suck it up as if not having parents
Is the same as living with
Three cars and vacations overseas
And owning everything you need or don't.

Suck it up
Like a black hole
Until we're left with nothing inside.

To Leave or Die in Nashville

But don't tell me that nothing
Hurts less than
Sticks and stones.
Don't tell me broken bones
Are a suitable substitute
For the names that follow
Your whole life and
Believing that every word is true.

Believing that what you are
Really is fat and that
The world really does hate you because
Someone said so and
Someone else agreed just to
Fit in and maybe feel cool for a bit,
Because it's better you than he
To be getting hit with
Every name they've ever thought of.

Sticks and stones hurt
That much is true
But they're better than
The hand grenades smuggled
Under tongues every day
And exploded in the battlefield
Of school halls.

Sticks and stones heal
Faster than the scars.
The bitter resentment
Ingrained inside of a personality
Until being subhuman is just
A definition for your own humanity.

Suck it up because they've
Never understood how his words
Can drive you to a point
Where the living breathing beating

Jeff Ryan

Part of existence becomes a chore
And it would be easier to be
Turned off.
And they laugh at his jokes
Because they've never hated him so much
That they turned into dogs
Ready to rip out a throat
And make him bleed or
Sharks looking to score a
Fix and kill something.

They've never hated like
You have.
They've never had to grow up
Thinking he was right.

But he wasn't.

You've got to remember
That stupid reason that made you
Keep trying
Even though everyone told you to quit
And all the shit you've been through
Is just a reminder that
They were wrong.
We are not what we were called.
We are the champions of the world
And inside of that truth
Is that motivation to keep going.

Because somewhere there is something
Beautiful to be loved
And somewhere there is a person
With callouses on his heart
Shouting they
Were
Wrong.

Evolution

Think of all
The millions of
Monkeys that died
So you could breathe.
The chimpanzees
And gorillas and grandparents
That led to
You
Sitting there
Numb and
Unbreathing.

Think of the
Atoms from Caesar's
Dying breath
In the lungs of
A gas station attendant
In Pennsylvania
Busy attending to gas
And cars of people
Lost trying to find
The interstate.

And then one day he drives
With the top of his car
Down into the fields
And looks at the moon
And eats a bullet
Because the world was
Just too grating.
Then the atoms from his
Last breath
Mix up
With the atoms from
Caesar's

And merge with you
As you're trying to end it
Again.

Elle

Don't ask me why I was there
I'll lie
Or come up with some other reason
Why I was only visiting.
But it's true that I fell in love
In a place where the
Sheets were sterile
And where they watched me like
God watches Christian boys
When they take cold showers.

She came in on the
Third day to a chorus
Of whispers, some welcome
Some not.
But she was gorgeous
Like Mary
Only her name was Elle
And right away
You could tell
That chick was a
Train wreck
Or a train stop
That took a rain check
And wasn't going to
Whirlwind into your
Life a second time.

She had this laugh like cocaine
And a way of talking
Like a ball of string unwinding
And even under her
Red hoodie you could tell
She was too skinny
In a way that made me want

Jeff Ryan

To save her.
Like a real sexy damsel
In distress.

While everyone else was
Content to whisper
I walked up to her and said,
"Hi
My name's Jeff."

She looked me up and
Looked me down and said,
"I haven't seen you here
Before and I've been here
Enough times to see everyone.

But you're cute."

And just like that
I felt like a human for the
First time since I'd died.
For the first time since
My heart had stopped beating
And I spent fifteen seconds
Proving there was no heaven
I remembered that I was a
Person who could smile
And that was the first
Miracle that Elle ever gave me.

Elle reads my poems
Though back then they're
Just mishmashes
And broken-hearted ballads.
She puts her hand
On mine
But does it
Under the table

To Leave or Die in Nashville

When no one's looking because
We were told pretty clearly
There's to be no fraternizing.

She tells me
Love's not such a bad thing
As I say in those poems. That
The sting you get can bring
Something amazing if you have
The patience to wait it out.

Back in those days I
Had a limp because my
Left leg stopped working
At the knee failing me
More by the day.
The point is I walked
So slow that I was sure
Love would be able to
Catch up to me just fine
In time.

Elle smiles in a way
The FDA should regulate.
She tells me she wants to
Be a writer if she grows up
Because there are stories
In her soul
Just begging to come out.

She tells me that
Family is just a
State of mind.
That it's too easy
To say I'll be yours
And you can be mine.
But then she tells me
We could do that anyways

Jeff Ryan

If we wanted.

She tells me
You've got to put
Your best foot forward first
So you can weather
The worst together.
It's got to be together.
Then she showed me the
Picture she drew me
Of a heart with my
Name in it
Made with crayon.

I still have it
In my room
Half a decade later
Ripped and fading.
I told her hearts were
Important because in
The end we all have to
Wear our wounds in our
Chests
Like medals on our uniforms
And she said
Not to be too proud of
All the casualties
And never act like a
Casualty again.
You have to do your best and
No matter what you have
To try.

My left leg means I'll never
Be a prize fighter or
Marathon runner but
I'd still pick myself up and
Parade through the streets

To Leave or Die in Nashville

Of Golgotha just to give her a
Day of rest. If that made
A difference.
I'd still try
Still take all the words
Inside me and some nearby
And do my best impression
Of a savior.
Even though I'm the barely scraping by
Son of a
Broken Hearted man and woman
Who couldn't tell you why
Some homeless men scream
That the end is nigh
But still waste it
On street corners
Yelling with their signs.

If it really is the end of days
Or when it does come calling
I won't care so much
About love or signs.
I'll just want to
Leave this world with
My face in a lock
Of her dirty blonde hair.

I told her, If I could I would
Write you something beautiful
Because I should because you're
Beautiful in a
Beautiful kind of way.

And she said back,
"That's sweet of you
But there's beauty
Everywhere
Like whenever

Jeff Ryan

It snows someone
Has to say it's snowing
And we all jolt our heads
Towards the window
As if we've never seen the
Sky drop white.

And that's why you have to live
Truly live
Not just breathing
Seconds into weeks
Even a year sneaks
Up if you close your
Eyes too long.
You'll keep beating yourself
Up trying to find
Beauty only in
Beautiful things.

There's beauty in a
Kickball game
Behind these walls
Because we can't have
Shoelaces so
If you kick the ball
At all really
Your shoes fall and fly
And you know our gym teacher
Would rather be in a
High school anywhere
That wasn't here,
Stuck with us.
There's a funny kind of
Beauty in that, too.

So listen,
I don't want to be beautiful
In any special kind of way.

To Leave or Die in Nashville

I'm just hoping that
Some piece of me gets
Shared and some piece of
Me gets remembered and
Some piece of me mattered
To someone else."

Elle
I wish that you could
Read these words.
I wish that you were still
Here instead of
Sitting six feet under the
Ground I live on.
Even though every day it
Gets harder to move
On my left leg
I swear I'd sprint
The second I saw you.
But it was true
When I told you I
Would try to do my
Very best to live.

I just wish I'd thought
To make you promise the same.

Jeff Ryan

To Leave or Die in Nashville

There's a library card in my
Wallet for
Welles-Turner Library
Back in a quiet town
In Connecticut.
I must owe them about
Thirty dollars.

I doubt that I'll pay it back.

They charged me fines for
Checking out books
Then disappearing
And it's just sort of
Stacked up ever since.
I heard they have
Forgiveness for half your fine
If you can find your books
And give them back
But I doubt it's worth
The trouble.

I'd rather just
Never use the card again.

Maybe I could have been some
Plantation heir and
Walked girls home
Between stalks of corn
And married my high
School girlfriend.

It would have been a life.

Instead I grew up

To Leave or Die in Nashville

Around churches made of
Wood and puritan blood
And houses with mismatched bricks.

I grew up smoking
Cigarettes behind
Chinese restaurants
And punching people I
Didn't like.

I grew up with a lot of hate
And never did learn how to
Not hold a grudge.

But things changed.
Now I wear shorts
In December
And kiss girls who sing
Country music.
Now I live in a mask
Making up the memories in between.

It's not a home
Any more than New England was.

But I had to leave or die.
I'm sorry.

Epilogue

One day I won't exist
Except within scratches etched
By blue pens onto
Pieces of paper.
My consciousness
Won't be
Anything but the chemicals
That fire in your brain
To read the symbols
Put down here.

But listen.
It was I who wrote this.

While you were out living,
Maybe doing your work
Or talking to girls
You wanted to kiss
Or learning about
How to cure sickness
I was sitting alone
With my pen and my book.

But even more importantly
Within these pages
Those I've known can live too.
It was said once
By some poet who was a little
Faster on the draw than I
That you die twice.
Once when you stop breathing
And again when someone says your name
For the last time.

So this thing, this is actually
A magic opportunity to
Make people live again
And a chance to take

Everything and everyone
I love and capture them
Through lenses of loneliness
And longing and memory.

I hope people say the name Elle forever.
Elle and DJ and Monica and Michelle
And all the people I've ever known and
All the people I've ever lost.

Poetry is selfish
Like that.

About the Author

Jeff Ryan was born in Hartford, Connecticut in 1993. After growing up in East Hartford and Glastonbury, he moved to Nashville to attend Vanderbilt University. He is currently working to obtain his undergraduate degree.

His first collection of poetry, *Chain Letters and Other Poems* became the #2 best-selling poetry book on Amazon and won acclaim from the University of Colorado's *Palimpsest Journal*. *To Leave or Die in Nashville* is his second work.

For more information, visit the author's website at jeffryanwriting.wordpress.com. Jeff can be reached at jffryan@gmail.com, or you can follow him on twitter at twitter.com/jryan2028.

Acknowledgements

How do I possibly thank everyone who helped make this book possible? I guess I have to start by thanking my parents for allowing me to do what I love in a city that I love. They know better than anyone how little money I make through writing...

Next I would like to thank everyone who purchased *Chain Letters* and made it such a success. Because of you all, I was able to get my foot in the door and get noticed enough to make this book possible – a real book in paper! Of course along with that I have to thank James Kinney for reaching out to me and all the other fine folks at Broken Lamp Publishers who worked with me at quite literally all hours of the day to hammer this thing out.

Finally, I would like to thank everyone else who helped turn my dream career into a possibility (and everyone who would get mad if they weren't thrown in somewhere). Jacelyn Szkrybalo, for being my editor and generally putting up with me; Kendra Osborn, for giving me the push to begin publishing and the momentum to keep it up; Rizzo, for being one of the best friends I've ever had; To Peabody, for being the other; Combs, for being just enough of an ass to make me a better writer; Haley, for being a friend in New England; Leah, for giving me a reason to come home; Brit Willson (she knows why); Niki Heller, and of course, to Emily.

Jeff Ryan
Nashville, TN

www.ingramcontent.com/pod-product-compliance
Lightning Source LLC
Chambersburg PA
CBHW071300040426
42444CB00009B/1811